RIVER SONGS

Selections from the Psalms
in the New King James Version

Text by
Jill and Stuart Briscoe

Thomas Nelson Publishers
Nashville · Camden · New York

Photo:	Page
Stockphotos international:	Forside, 30-31,52-53,72-73
Robert C. Hayes:	4-5,22,63,65,68
Urpu A. Tarnanen:	6-7,10-11,14-15,26,27,36,37, 44,45,62,69,76,77,78-79
Explorer:	8-9,
Joachim Kinkelin:	12-13,34-35
G. Grønbeck:	16,
Photo Solbjerghøj:	17,
Bavaria:	18-19,
Alan Bedding:	20-21,
R. Rauth:	23,42-43,50-51,70-71
Wilfred Konrad:	24-25,
Otto Wikkelsø:	28,
Tony Stone Ass.:	29,32-33,54-55,64
Willy P. Burkhardt:	38-39,
Scandinavia:	40,41,46,47,49,58-59, 66-67,
Peter Østergrens:	48,
G + M Kohler:	56,
Bildarchiv Huber:	57,
Löbl-Schreyer:	60-61,
Zefa:	74-75,
Walter Geiersperger:	80.

Published in Nashville, Tennessee, by Thomas Nelson, Inc., and distributed in Canada by Lawson Falle, Ltd., Cambridge, Ontario.

Text selections followed by the initials JB are by Jill Briscoe.
Text selections followed by the initials SB are by Stuart Briscoe.

ISBN 0-8407-5366-7

Printed in Singapore by Tien Wah Press (PTE) Ltd

RIVER SONGS
Selections from the Psalms

*He split the
rocks in the wilderness,
And gave them drink in abundance
like the depths. He also brought
streams out of the rock,
And caused waters
to run down
like rivers.*

But as for me, my prayer is to You, O Lord, in the acceptable time; O God, in the multitude of Your mercy, hear me in the truth of Your salvation. Deliver me out of the mire, and let me not sink; let me be delivered from those who hate me, and out of the deep waters. Let not the floodwater overflow me, nor let the deep swallow me up; and let not the pit shut its mouth on

*me. Hear me, O L*ORD*, for Your lovingkindness is good; turn to me according to the multitude of Your tender mercies. And do not hide Your face from Your servant, for I am in trouble; hear me speedily. Draw near to my soul and redeem it; deliver me because of my enemies.*

A Father to the Fatherless

Let God arise,
Let His enemies be scattered;
Let those also who hate Him
flee before Him.
As smoke is driven away,
So drive them away;
As wax melts before the fire,
So let the wicked perish
at the presence of God.
But let the righteous be glad;
Let them rejoice before God;
Yes, let them rejoice exceedingly.
Sing to God, sing praises to His name;
Extol Him who rides on the clouds,
By His name YAH, and rejoice before Him.
A father of the fatherless,
a defender of widows,
Is God in His holy habitation.
God sets the solitary in families;
He brings out those who are bound
into prosperity;
But the rebellious dwell in a dry land.
O God, when You went out before Your people,
When You marched through the wilderness,
The earth shook;
The heavens also dropped rain at the presence of God;
Sinai itself was moved at the presence of God,
the God of Israel.
You, O God, sent a plentiful rain,
Whereby You confirmed Your inheritance,
When it was weary.
Your congregation dwelt in it;
You, O God, provided from Your goodness for the poor.

[verses 1–10]

*Thank you Father that You invented families
so that we need never be lonely and might
learn how to be unselfish. But life
being what it is, death intervenes
and wives become widows and children
find themselves fatherless.
When this happens, Lord, You prove
Yourself again, and we rejoice in Your care.*—SB

God Reigns from High Places

The Lord gave the word;
Great was the company of those who proclaimed it:
"Kings of armies flee, they flee,
And she who remains at home divides the spoil.
Though you lie down among the sheepfolds,
Yet you will be like the wings of a dove
covered with silver,
And her feathers with yellow gold."
When the Almighty scattered kings in it,
It was white as snow in Zalmon.
A mountain of God is the mountain of Bashan;
A mountain of many peaks is the mountain of Bashan.
Why do you fume with envy, you mountains
of many peaks?
This is the mountain which God desires to dwell in;
Yes, the LORD will dwell in it forever.
The chariots of God are twenty thousand,
Even thousands of thousands;
The Lord is among them as in Sinai; in the Holy Place.
You have ascended on high,
You have led captivity captive;
You have received gifts among men,
Even among the rebellious,
That the LORD God might dwell there.
Blessed be the Lord, who daily loads us with benefits;
The God of our salvation!
Our God is the God of salvation;
And to GOD the Lord belong escapes from death.

[verses 11–20]

*When I look at the rugged mountains towering
majestically over the valleys, I'm reminded of
the throne of the Lord from which He rules in
glory and righteousness. I think of the risen
Lord, ascending to the Father's throne, leading
in a glorious parade—those whom He delivered
from death. And I rejoice that He has given me
a place with Him in glory.—SB*

Proclaim the Power Of God

But God will wound the head of His enemies,
The hairy scalp of the one who still goes on
in His trespasses.
The Lord said, "I will bring back from Bashan,
I will bring them back from the depths of the sea,
That your foot may crush them in blood,
And the tongues of your dogs may have their portion
from your enemies."
They have seen your procession, O God,
The procession of my God, my King, into the sanctuary.
The singers went before, the players on instruments
followed after;
Among them were the maidens playing timbrels.
Bless God in the congregations,
The Lord, from the fountain of Israel.
There is little Benjamin, their leader,
The princes of Judah and their company,
The princes of Zebulun and the princes of Naphtali.
Your God has commanded your strength;
Strengthen, O God, what You have done for us.
Because of your temple at Jerusalem,
Kings will bring presents to You.
Rebuke the beasts of the reeds,
The herd of bulls with the calves of the peoples,
Till everyone submits himself with pieces of silver.
Scatter the peoples who delight in war.
Envoys will come out of Egypt;
Ethiopia will quickly stretch out her hands to God.
Sing to God, you kingdoms of the earth;
Oh, sing praises to the Lord,
To Him who rides on the heaven of heavens,
which were of old!
Indeed, He sends out His voice, a mighty voice.
Ascribe strength to God; His excellence is over Israel,
And His strength is in the clouds.
O God, You are more awesome than Your holy places.
The God of Israel is He who gives strength and power
to His people. Blessed be God!

[verses 21–35]

Lord, I have to see evidences of Your power.
Anything that reminds me of Your strength
spreads deeply to my soul. For Your power is
not an academic concept—it is a divine
dynamic, made available to all Your people to
equip them for service and lifestyle that honor
You.—SB

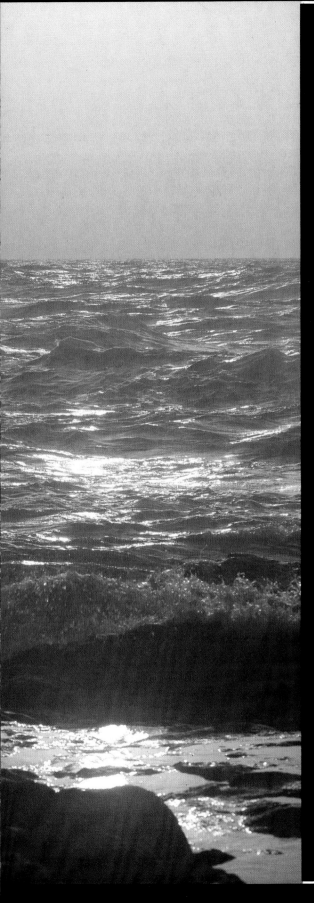

From PSALM 69

Save Me, O God

Save me, O God!
For the waters have come up to my neck.
I sink in deep mire, where there is no standing;
I have come into deep waters,
Where the floods overflow me.
I am weary with my crying;
My throat is dry;
My eyes fail while I wait for my God.
Those who hate me without a cause
Are more than the hairs of my head;
They are mighty who would destroy me,
Being my enemies wrongfully;
Though I have stolen nothing,
I still must restore it.
O God, You know my foolishness;
And my sins are not hidden from You.
Let not those who wait for You,
O Lord GOD of hosts, be ashamed because of me;
Let not those who seek You be confounded
because of me,
O God of Israel.
Because for Your sake I have borne reproach;
Shame has covered my face.
I have become a stranger to my brothers,
And an alien to my mother's children;
Because zeal for Your house has eaten me up,
And the reproaches of those who reproach You
have fallen on me.
When I wept and chastened my soul with fasting,
That became my reproach.
I also made sackcloth my garment;
I became a byword to them.
Those who sit in the gate speak against me,
And I am the song of the drunkards.
But as for me, my prayer is to You,
O LORD, in the acceptable time;
O God, in the multitude of Your mercy,
Hear me in the truth of Your salvation.

[verses 1–13]

When I'm in over my head, engulfed in
floods of criticism—
when I'm worn out with worry and I become
the family joke—
when people make fun of me and I weep
alone—
Then I'm comforted by knowing—
THIS IS FOR YOU!—JB

ome Near and Rescue Me

liver me out of the mire, and let me not sink;
: me be delivered from those who hate me,
d out of the deep waters.
: not the floodwater overflow me,
r let the deep swallow me up;
d let not the pit shut its mouth on me.
ar me, O LORD, for Your lovingkindness is good;
rn to me according to the multitude
Your tender mercies.
d do not hide Your face from Your servant,
: I am in trouble; hear me speedily.
aw near to my soul, and redeem it;
liver me because of my enemies.
u know my reproach, my shame,
d my dishonor;
/ adversaries are all before You.
proach has broken my heart,
d I am full of heaviness;
ooked for someone to take pity,
t there was none;
d for comforters, but I found none.
ey also gave me gall for my food,
d for my thirst they gave me vinegar to drink.
: their table become a snare before them,
d their well-being a trap.
: their eyes be darkened, so that they do not see;
d make their loins shake continually.
ur out Your indignation upon them,
d let Your wrathful anger take hold of them.
: their habitation be desolate;
: no one dwell in their tents.
r they persecute him whom You have struck,
d talk of the grief of those You have wounded.
d iniquity to their iniquity,
d let them not come into Your righteousness.
: them be blotted out of the book of the living,
d not be written with the righteous.

[verses 14–28]

oken heart and heavy spirit,
ne to care, encourage, smile;
ft me up and help me merit,
d's good pleasure in a while!
ar my prayer—attend my sorrow,
d of past and black tomorrow.
d will save me, God will keep me.
d will make it all worthwhile!—JB

You Are My Deliverer

Make haste, O God, to deliver me!
Make haste to help me, O Lord!
Let them be ashamed and confounded who seek my
life;
Let them be turned back and confused who desire my
hurt.
Let them be turned back because of their shame,
Who say, "Aha, aha!"
Let all those who seek You rejoice and be glad in You;
And let those who love Your salvation say continually,
"Let God be magnified!"
But I am poor and needy;
Make haste to me, O God!
You are my help and my deliverer;
O Lord, do not delay.

*David asked God to hurry. Have you ever asked
God to hurry up and answer your prayers?
Christian character isn't produced in a hurry.
When Lazarus was sick, Martha and Mary
couldn't understand why Jesus, knowing the
situation, stayed where he was. If the Lord had
hurried to their side they would never have seen
their brother raised from the dead and
understood that Christ is the resurrection and
the life!—JB*

From PSALM 71

My Confidence Since My Youth

In You, O LORD, I put my trust;
Let me never be put to shame.
Deliver me in Your righteousness,
and cause me to escape;
Incline Your ear to me, and save me.
Be my strong habitation,
To which I may resort continually;
You have given the commandment to save me,
For You are my rock and my fortress.
Deliver me, O my God,
out of the hand of the wicked,
Out of the hand of the unrighteous and cruel man
For You are my hope, O Lord GOD;
You are my trust from my youth.
By You I have been upheld from my birth;
You are He who took me
out of my mother's womb.
My praise shall be continually of You.
I have become as a wonder to many,
But You are my strong refuge.
Let my mouth be filled with Your praise
And with Your glory all the day.
Do not cast me off in the time of old age;
Do not forsake me when my strength fails.
For my enemies speak against me;
And those who lie in wait for my life
take counsel together,
Saying, "God has forsaken him;
Pursue and take him,
for there is none to deliver him."
O God, do not be far from me;
O my God, make haste to help me!
Let them be confounded and consumed
Who are adversaries of my life;
Let them be covered with reproach and dishonor
Who seek my hurt.

[verses 1–13]

Men talk about provision made by society from "womb to tomb"! They fondly imagine they can meet every human need. But you, Lord, knew me before I came forth from the womb, and when I am old and go to my tomb, then I shall go to be with You. And in between, I know You stand by me.—SB

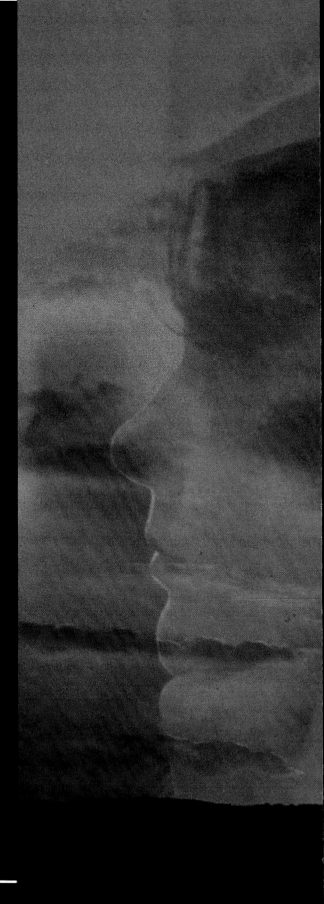

I Will Ever Praise You

But I will hope continually,
And will praise You yet more and more.
My mouth shall tell of Your righteousness
And Your salvation all the day.
For I do not know their limits.
I will go in the strength of the Lord GOD;
I will make mention of Your righteousness,
of Yours only.
O God, You have taught me from my youth;
And to this day I declare Your wondrous works.
Now also when I am old and grayheaded,
O God, do not forsake me,
Until I declare Your strength to this generation,
Your power to everyone who is to come.
Also Your righteousness, O God, is very high,
You who have done great things;
O God, who is like You?
You, who have shown me great and severe troubles,
Shall revive me again,
And bring me up again from the depths of the earth.
You shall increase my greatness,
And comfort me on every side.
Also with the lute I will praise you—
And Your faithfulness, O my God!
To You I will sing with the harp,
O Holy One of Israel.
My lips shall greatly rejoice when I sing to You,
And my soul, which You have redeemed.
My tongue also shall talk of Your righteousness
all the day long;
For they are confounded,
For they are brought to shame
Who seek my hurt.

[verses 14–24]

*I will never cease to thank You, Lord, that I
learned about You in my youth. Through life's
changing scenes, I have consistently proved
Your righteousness and faithfulness, and I have
known all my life that when my days will come
to an end You will revive me and take me to
glory. Truly, O God, who is like You?—SB*

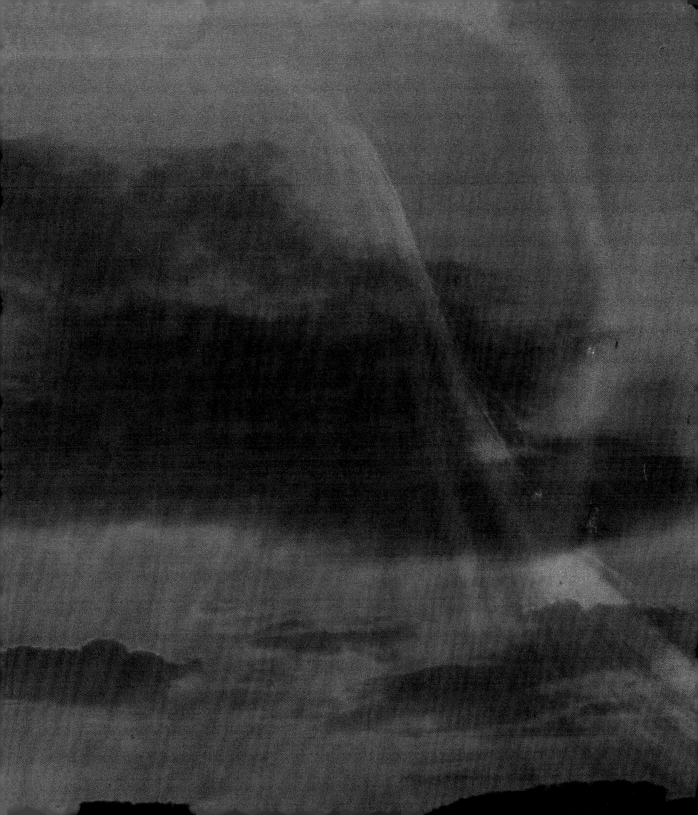

The Royal Son

Give the king Your judgments, O God,
And your righteousness to the king's Son.
He will judge Your people with righteousness,
And your poor with justice.
The mountains will bring peace to the people,
And the little hills, by righteousness.
He will bring justice to the poor of the people;
He will save the children of the needy,
And will break in pieces the oppressor.
They shall fear You
As long as the sun and moon endure,
Throughout all generations.
He shall come down like rain
upon the mown grass,
Like showers that water the earth.
In His days the righteous shall flourish,
And abundance of peace,
Until the moon is no more.
He shall have dominion also from sea to sea,
And from the River to the ends of the earth.
Those who dwell in the wilderness
will bow before Him,
And His enemies will lick the dust.
The kings of Tarshish and of the isles
Will bring presents;
The kings of Sheba and Seba will offer gifts.
Yes, all kings shall fall down before Him;
All nations shall serve Him.

[verses 1–11]

This psalm gives us a vision of the righteou
character of Messiah's kingdom. Can you
imagine what it will be like to feel all righ
live in a world that's all right, with people
who are all right? The poor will be rich,
the children of the needy will have plenty,
and the nations will serve Him together.
That Kingdom is the Son's Royal Right!—ji

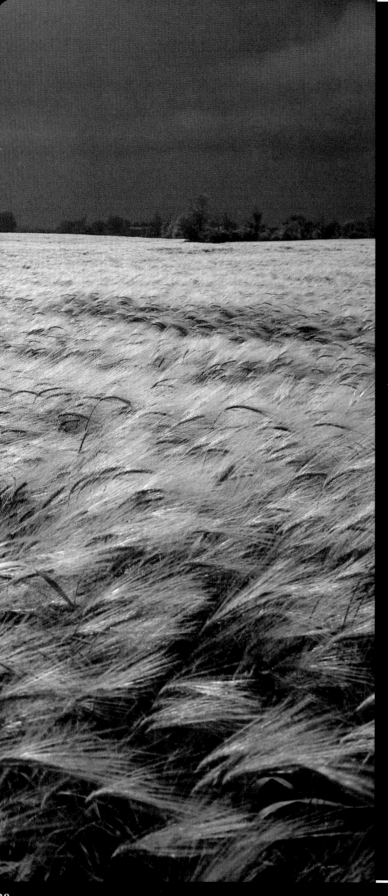

May the Earth Be Filled with His Glory

For He will deliver the needy when he cries,
The poor also, and him who has no helper.
He will spare the poor and needy,
And will save the souls of the needy.
He will redeem their life from oppression
and violence;
And precious shall be their blood in His sight.
And He shall live;
And the gold of Sheba will be given to Him;
Prayer also will be made for Him continually,
And daily He shall be praised.
There will be an abundance of grain in the earth,
On the top of the mountains;
Its fruit shall wave like Lebanon;
And those of the city shall flourish like
grass of the earth.
His name shall endure forever;
His name shall continue as long as the sun.
And men shall be blessed in Him;
All nations shall call Him blessed.
Blessed be the LORD God, the God of Israel,
Who only does wondrous things!
And blessed be His glorious name forever!
And let the whole earth be filled with His glory.
Amen and Amen.
The prayers of David the son of Jesse are ended.

[verses 12–20]

Kings of the earth come and go, but our King will live forever! All kings will bow before our King, but He will lift them up, accept their gifts, and give a decree in all the earth!
"Deliver, spare, redeem the helpless—precious is their blood in my sight."
Oh, precious King—Come!—JB

In God's Sanctuary

Truly God is good to Israel,
To such as are pure in heart,
But as for me, my feet had almost stumbled;
My steps had nearly slipped.
For I was envious of the boastful,
When I saw the prosperity of the wicked.
For there are no pangs in their death,
But their strength is firm.
They are not in trouble as other men,
Nor are they plagued like other men.
Therefore pride serves as their necklace;
Violence covers them like a garment.
Their eyes bulge with abundance;
They have more than heart could wish.
They scoff and speak wickedly concerning oppression;
They speak loftily.
They set their mouth against the heavens,
And their tongue walks through the earth.
Therefore his people return here,
And waters of a full cup are drained by them.
And they say, "How does God know?
And is there knowledge in the Most High?"
Behold, these are the ungodly,
Who are always at ease;
They increase in riches.
Surely I have cleansed my heart in vain,
And washed my hands in innocence.
For all day long I have been plagued,
And chastened every morning.
If I had said, "I will speak thus,"
Behold, I would have been untrue to the
generation of Your children.
When I thought how to understand this,
It was too painful for me—
Until I went into the sanctuary of God;
Then I understood their end.

[verses 1–17]

*Life is a slippery slope. Particularly in the area
of attitudes. I have had trouble with envy as I
have watched others prosper while I was
impoverished. At times I have become cynical,
even to the point of doubting You, Lord. And
that is a slippery slope—but You kept me from
falling and for that I am grateful.—SB*

The Strength of My Heart

Surely You set them in slippery places;
You cast them down to destruction.
Oh, how they are brought to desolation,
as in a moment!
They are utterly consumed with terrors.
As a dream when one awakes,
So, Lord, when You awake,
You shall despise their image.
Thus my heart was grieved,
And I was vexed in my mind.
I was so foolish and ignorant;
I was like a beast before You.
Nevertheless I am continually with You;
You hold me by my right hand.
You will guide me with Your counsel,
And afterward receive me to glory.
Whom have I in heaven but You?
And there is none upon earth that I desire
besides You.
My flesh and my heart fail;
But God is the strength of my heart
and my portion forever.
For indeed, those who are far from You
shall perish;
You have destroyed all those who desert You
for harlotry.
But it is good for me to draw near to God;
I have put my trust in the Lord GOD,
That I may declare all Your works.

[verses 18–28]

People and problems keep me earthbound. My thinking and my actions so often betray an orientation to this world rather than heaven—to the material rather than the spiritual. But then I remember to take wings to Your presence, and I remember how good it is for me to be near God.—SB

From PSALM 74

Rise Against Your Enemy

O God, why have You cast us off forever?
Why does Your anger smoke against the sheep
of Your pasture?
Remember Your congregation,
which You have purchased of old,
The tribe of Your inheritance,
which You have redeemed—
This Mount Zion where You have dwelt.
Lift up Your feet to the perpetual desolations.
The enemy has damaged everything in the sanctuary.
Your enemies roar in the midst of Your meeting place;
They set up their banners for signs.
They seem like men who lift up axes among the
thick trees.
And now they break down its carved work, all at once,
with axes and hammers,
They have set fire to Your sanctuary;
They have defiled the dwelling place of Your name
to the ground.
They said in their hearts,
"Let us destroy them altogether."
They have burned up all the meeting places of God
in the land.
We do not see our signs;
There is no longer any prophet;
Nor is there any among us who knows how long.
O God, how long will the adversary reproach?
Will the enemy blaspheme Your name forever?
Why do You withdraw Your hand, even Your right hand?
Take it out of Your bosom and destroy them.

[verses 1–11]

Asaph contemplates national and spiritual disaster, and wonders if "it is all over." No prophet prophesies, God's house is in ruins, His right hand is still. Do you ever wonder if "it is all over?" "God is not there," you lament, "He is silent!" Asaph learned that God is never silent—quiet perhaps—but biding His time to arise and come to our help!—JB

ise and Defend Your Cause

r God is my King from of old,
orking salvation in the midst of the earth.
ou divided the sea by Your strength;
ou broke the heads of the sea serpents
 the waters.
ou broke the heads of Leviathan in pieces,
nd gave him as food to the people inhabiting
e wilderness.
ou broke open the fountain and the flood;
ou dried up mighty rivers,
ie day is Yours, the night also is Yours;
ou have prepared the light and the sun.
ou have set all the borders of the earth;
ou have made summer and winter.
member this, that the enemy has
proached, O LORD,
nd that a foolish people
s blasphemed Your name.
n, do not deliver the life of Your turtledove
 the wild beast!
 not forget the life of Your poor forever.
ave respect to the covenant;
r the dark places of the earth are full of
e inhabitations of cruelty.
n, do not let the oppressed return ashamed!
t the poor and needy praise Your name.
ise, O God, plead Your own cause;
member how the foolish man
proaches You daily.
 not forget the voice of Your enemies;
ie tumult of those who rise up against You
creases continually.

[verses 12–23]

od sends us forth doves among
redators—sheep among wolves, that He
ight come to our aid. When helpless
eople lean on their Helper and learn to
and upright and face the odds against
em, God remembers His promises. God
mes through and so do we!—JB

*You broke open
the fountain and the flood;
You dried up mighty rivers.*

raise to God

e give thanks to You, O God, we give thanks!
r Your wondrous works declare that
ur name is near.
When I choose the proper time,
will judge uprightly.
he earth and all its inhabitants are dissolved;
set up its pillars firmly.   Selah
said to the boastful, "Do not deal boastfully,"
nd to the wicked, "Do not lift up the horn.
o not lift up your horn on high;
o not speak with a stiff neck."
r exaltation comes neither from the east
or from the west nor from the south.
ut God is the Judge; He puts down one,
d exalts another.
r in the hand of the Lord there is a cup,
nd the wine is red;
is fully mixed, and He pours it out;
urely its dregs shall all the wicked of the earth
ain and drink down.
ut I will declare forever,
will sing praises to the God of Jacob.
ll the horns of the wicked I will also cut off,
ut the horns of the righteous shall be exalted."

ou give us freedom, Lord, to humbly
raise You or arrogantly resist You. Even
om our earliest days, this is apparent.
ut our own freedom ends, for You exalt
hose who humble themselves and
umble those who exalt themselves.—SB

Who Can Stand Before God?

In Judah God is known;
His name is great in Israel,
In Salem also is His tabernacle,
And His dwelling place in Zion.
There He broke the arrows of the bow,
the shield and the sword and the battle-ax.　　Selah
You are more glorious and excellent
Than the mountains of prey.
The stouthearted were plundered;
They have sunk into their sleep;
And none of the mighty men
have found the use of their hands.
At Your rebuke, O God of Jacob, both the chariot
and horse were cast into a dead sleep.
You, Yourself, are to be feared;
And who may stand in Your presence
When once You are angry?
You caused judgment to be heard from heaven;
The earth feared and was still,
when God arose to judgment,
To deliver all the oppressed of the earth.　　Selah
Surely the wrath of man shall praise You;
With the remainder of wrath You shall gird Yourself.
Make vows to the LORD your God, and pay them;
Let all who are around Him bring presents to Him
who ought to be feared.
He shall cut off the spirit of princes;
He is awesome to the kings of the earth.

*What animal can match the horse for nobility
and dignity? Flowing mane, glistening flanks,
dilated nostrils, pricked ears, straining neck,
smooth muscles all combine in magnificent
symmetry. But even the fearsome warhorse can
be stopped in its tracks—more importantly,
your Lord can make wars to cease and
hostilities to end.—SB*

our Ways, O God

ried out to God with my voice—
God with my voice; and He gave ear to me.
the day of my trouble I sought the Lord;
y hand was stretched out in the night
thout ceasing;
y soul refused to be comforted. . . .
ill the Lord cast off forever?
nd will He be favorable no more?
as His mercy ceased forever?
as His promise failed forevermore?
as God forgotten to be gracious?
as He in anger shut up His tender mercies?
nd I said, "This is my anguish;
t I will remember the years of the right hand
the Most High."
will remember the works of the LORD;
rely I will remember Your wonders of old.
will also meditate on all Your work,
nd talk of Your deeds.
ur way, O God, is in the sanctuary;
ho is so great a God as our God?
u are the God who does wonders;
u have declared Your strength among the peoples.
u have with Your arm redeemed Your people,
e sons of Jacob and Joseph.   Selah
e waters saw you, O God;
e waters saw you, they were afraid;
e depths also trembled.
e clouds poured out water;
e skies sent out a sound;
ur arrows also flashed about.
e voice of Your thunder was in the whirlwind;
e lightnings lit up the world;
e earth trembled and shook.
ur way was in the sea,
ur path in the great waters,
nd your footsteps were not known.
u led Your people like a flock
the hand of Moses and Aaron.

od gives us songs in the night! We find
easy to hum a dandy ditty while it's
y; songs in the night come harder! My
irit will have to search the darkness
r memories of mercy. Like Asaph, faith
ill help me cry, "Who is so great a God
our God?"—JB

45

ell of the Deeds of the Lord

ve ear, O my people, to my law;
cline your ears to the words of my mouth.
will open my mouth in a parable;
will utter dark sayings of old,
hich we have heard and known,
d our fathers have told us.
e will not hide them from their children,
lling to the generation to come the praises
the LORD,
d His strength and His wonderful works
at He has done.
r He established a testimony in Jacob,
d appointed a law in Israel,
hich He commanded our fathers, . . .
at they may arise and declare them
their children,
at they may set their hope in God,
d not forget the works of God,
t keep His commandments;
d may not be like their fathers,
stubborn and rebellious generation,
generation that did not set its heart aright,
d whose spirit was not faithful to God.
e children of Ephraim, being armed and carrying
ws, turned back in the day of battle.
ey did not keep the covenant of God;
ey refused to walk in His law,
d forgot His works
d His wonders that he had shown them.
arvelous things He did in the sight of their fathers,
the land of Egypt, in the field of Zoan.
e divided the sea and caused them to pass through;
d He made the waters stand up like a heap.
the daytime also he led them with the cloud,
d all the night with a light of fire.

[verses 1–14]

o you ever feel jealous when you hear
out a Godly heritage? "Why couldn't I
born in a Christian home?" you ask
od. "Start a Christian heritage," the
ther may reply. Marry a child of God
d begin teaching your children, praying
your grandchildren—yet to be
rn!—JB

From PSALM 78

Food in the Desert

He split the rocks in the wilderness,
And gave them drink in abundance like the depth
He also brought streams out of the rock,
And caused waters to run down like rivers.
But they sinned even more against Him
By rebelling against the Most High
in the wilderness.
And they tested God in their heart
By asking for the food of their fancy.
Yes, they spoke against God:
They said, "Can God prepare a table
in the wilderness?
Behold, He struck the rock,
So that the waters gushed out,
And the streams overflowed.
Can He give bread also?
Can He provide meat for His people?"
Therefore the Lord heard this and was furious;
So a fire was kindled against Jacob,
And anger also came up against Israel,
Because they did not believe in God,
And did not trust in His salvation.
Yet He had commanded the clouds above,
And opened the doors of heaven,
Had rained down manna on them to eat,
And given them of the bread of heaven.
Men ate angels' food;
He sent them food to the full.
He caused an east wind to blow in the heavens;
And by His power he brought in the south wind.
He also rained meat on them like the dust,
Feathered fowl like the sand of the seas;
And He let them fall in the midst of their camp,
All around their habitations.
So they ate and were well filled,
For He gave them their own desire.   [verses 15–29

*Whenever I'm tempted to question Your
ability, Lord, I check up on history. In
days of old You did wonderful things for
Your people in the wilderness—water
flowed from rocks at Your command,
manna fell from heaven at Your dictate.
Rivers still flow, waterfalls still roar—
daily reminders of the great God who
provides for His people.—SB*

The Sin of the People

They were not deprived of their craving;
But while their food was still in their mouth,
the wrath of God came against them,
and slew the stoutest of them,
And struck down the choice men of Israel.
In spite of this they still sinned,
And did not believe in His wondrous works.
Therefore their days He consumed in futility,
And their years in fear.
When He slew them, then they sought Him;
And they returned and sought diligently for God.
Then they remembered that God was their rock,
And the Most High God their redeemer.
Nevertheless they flattered Him with their mouth,
And they lied to Him with their tongue;
For their heart was not steadfast with Him,
Nor were they faithful in His covenant.
But He, being full of compassion,
forgave their iniquity,
And did not destroy them.
Yes, many a time He turned His anger away,
And did not stir up all His wrath;
For He remembered that they were but flesh,
A breath that passes away and does not come again.

[verses 30–39]

*Shifting sands, unstable and treacherous, so
often remind me of the unfaithfulness of man—
of fickleness and unreliability. But You stand
like a rock, Lord. You are consistent in Your
justice, unchanging in Your grace. When I
remember this I turn, repentant, to You,
desirous of pleasing You.—SB*

The Lord Guides His People

How often they provoked Him in the wilderness,
And grieved Him in the desert!
Yes, again and again they tempted God,
And limited the Holy One of Israel.
They did not remember His power:
The day when He redeemed them from the enemy,
When He worked His signs in Egypt,
And His wonders in the field of Zoan;
Turned their rivers into blood,
And their streams, that they could not drink.
He sent swarms of flies among them,
which devoured them,
And frogs, which destroyed them.
He also gave their crops to the caterpillar,
And their labor to the locust.
He destroyed their vines with hail,
And their sycamore trees with frost.
He also gave up their cattle to the hail,
And their flocks to fiery lightning.
He cast on them the fierceness of His anger,
Wrath, indignation, and trouble,
By sending angels of destruction among them.
He made a path for His anger;
He did not spare their soul from death,
But gave their life over to the plague,
And destroyed all the firstborn in Egypt,
The first of their strength in the tents of Ham.
But He made His own people go forth like sheep,
And guided them in the wilderness like a flock;
And He led them on safely, so that they did not fear;
But the sea overwhelmed their enemies.
And He brought them to His holy border,
This mountain which His right hand had acquired.
He also drove out the nations before them,
Allotted them an inheritance by survey,
And made the tribes of Israel dwell in their tents.

[verses 40–55]

*How soon we forget to say thank you! Israel
forgot, and in the forgetting frustrated their
Guide and King. When things look difficult for
the future, learn to say thank you for the past.
That sort of attitude can only bring you
deliverance in the present!—JB*

Save me, O God!
For the waters have come up
to my neck. I sink in deep mire,
where there is no standing; I have come
into deep waters, where the floods
overflow me.

From PSALM 78

The Fire of the Lord

Yet they tested and provoked the Most High God,
And did not keep His testimonies,
But turned back and acted unfaithfully
like their fathers;
They were turned aside like a deceitful bow.
For they provoked Him to anger with their
high places, and moved Him to jealousy
with their carved images. When God heard this,
He was furious, and greatly abhorred Israel, . . .
And delivered His strength into captivity,
And His glory into the enemy's hand.
He also gave His people over to the sword,
And was furious with His inheritance.
The fire consumed their young men,
And their maidens were not given in marriage.
Their priests fell by the sword,
And their widows made no lamentation.
Then the Lord awoke as one out of sleep,
And like a mighty man who shouts
because of wine.
And He beat back His enemies;
He put them to a perpetual reproach.
Moreover He rejected the tent of Joseph,
And did not choose the tribe of Ephraim,
But chose the tribe of Judah,
Mount Zion which he loved.
And He built His sanctuary like the heights,
Like the earth which He has established forever.
He also chose David His servant,
And took him from the sheepfolds; . . .
To shepherd Jacob His people,
and Israel His inheritance.
So he shepherded them according to the
integrity of his heart,
And guided them by the skillfulness of his hands
[verses 56–72]

*God took David from looking after sheep
and gave him people to shepherd instead.
Jesus took Peter from his fishing nets and
made him a fisher of men. God will use
the color of our culture to shape us for
the function of our future. When God
takes us from our daily doings to do a
work for Him, we shall find we are finely
equipped by the Master.—JB*

Then Our People Will Praise

O God, the nations have come into Your inheritance;
Your holy temple they have defiled;
They have laid Jerusalem in heaps.
The dead bodies of Your servants they have given
as food for the birds of the heavens,
The flesh of Your saints to the beasts of the earth.
Their blood they have shed like water all around
Jerusalem, and there was no one to bury them.
We have become a reproach to our neighbors,
A scorn and derision to those who are around us.
How long, Lord? Will You be angry forever?
Will Your jealousy burn like fire?
Pour out Your wrath on the nations
that do not know You,
And on the kingdoms that do not call on Your name.
For they have devoured Jacob,
And laid waste his dwelling place.
Oh, do not remember former iniquities against us!
Let Your tender mercies come speedily to meet us,
For we have been brought very low.
Help us, O God of our salvation,
For the glory of Your name;
And deliver us, and provide atonement for our sins,
For Your name's sake!
Why should the nations say, "Where is their God?"
Let there be known among the nations in our sight
The avenging of the blood of Your servants
which has been shed.
Let the groaning of the prisoner come before You;
According to the greatness of Your power
Preserve those who are appointed to die;
And return to our neighbors sevenfold into their bosom
Their reproach with which they have reproached You,
O Lord.
So we, Your people and sheep of Your pasture,
Will give You thanks forever;
We will show forth Your praise to all generations.

*The long sad history of Jerusalem testified
unmistakably to the sinfulness of God's people
and the righteous judgment of God. He has
never forsaken His people, neither has He let
their sin go unpunished. But always he has been
eager to aid the repentant and ready to show
mercy to those who call! For this His people
praise Him.*—SB

Shine Upon Us

Give ear, O Shepherd of Israel,
You who lead Joseph like a flock;
You who dwell between the cherubim, shine forth!
Before Ephraim, Benjamin, and Manasseh,
Stir up Your strength,
And come and save us!
Restore us, O God;
Cause Your face to shine,
And we shall be saved!
O LORD God of hosts,
How long will You be angry
Against the prayer of Your people?
You have fed them with the bread of tears,
And given them tears to drink in great measure.
You have made us a strife to our neighbors,
And our enemies laugh among themselves.
Restore us, O God of hosts;
Cause Your face to shine,
And we shall be saved!   [verses 1–7]

*That every cloud has a silver lining is a fond
imagination. Sometimes we peer long and hard
to see the shine—to glimpse the glow. But You
promise to shine on us in our distress, and in
Your light we see darkness disappear.—SB*

evive Us

turn, we beseech You,
God of hosts;
ok down from heaven and see,
d visit this vine
d the vineyard which Your
ht hand has planted,
d the branch that You
de strong for Yourself.
s burned with fire, it is cut down;
ey perish at the rebuke
Your countenance.
t Your hand be upon the man of Your
ht hand,
on the son of man
om You made strong for Yourself.
en we will not turn back from You;
vive us,
d we will call upon Your name.
store us, O LORD God of hosts;
use Your face to shine,
d we shall be saved!

[verses 14–19]

rael, God's vine planted deep in the
rtile soil of blessing, produced sweet
ine. But the vine made bad choices,
coming a degenerate plant—sour
apes ensued.
ristians are planted with God's
oicest vine—the Lord Jesus Christ—
at our cheerless world might celebrate.
t us take heed and learn the lesson of
e vine!—JB

od Our Strength

g aloud to God our strength;
ke a joyful shout to the God of Jacob.
ise a song and strike the timbrel,
e pleasant harp with the lute.
w the trumpet at the time of the New Moon,
the full moon, on our solemn feast day.
this is a statute for Israel,
d a law of the God of Jacob.
is He established in Joseph for a testimony,
en He went throughout the land of Egypt,
ere I heard a language that I did not understand.
moved his shoulder from the burden;
hands were freed from the baskets.
called in trouble, and I delivered you;
nswered you in the secret place of thunder;
roved you at the waters of Meribah.   Selah
ar, O My people, and I will admonish you!
Israel, if you will listen to Me!
ere shall be no foreign god among you;
r shall you worship any foreign god.
m the LORD your God,
ho brought you out of the land of Egypt;
en your mouth wide, and I will fill it,
t My people would not heed My voice,
d Israel would have none of Me.
I gave them over to their own stubborn heart,
walk in their own counsels.
, that My people would listen to Me,
at Israel would walk in My ways!
ould soon subdue their enemies,
d turn My hand against their adversaries.
e haters of the LORD would pretend
mission to Him,
t their fate would endure forever.
would have fed them also with
finest of wheat;
d with honey from the rock
ould have satisfied you.

*rael questioned God at Meribah. The
ople were thirsty and believed
emselves forsaken. They chided Moses
d they tempted God. It helps to think
God's mercy in time of doubt.
member your Meribahs—did not water
w from the Lord your Rock and
ench your thirst?—JB*

Rescue the Weak

God stands in the congregation of the mighty;
He judges among the gods.
How long will you judge unjustly,
And show partiality to the wicked?   Selah
Defend the poor and fatherless;
Do justice to the afflicted and needy.
Deliver the poor and needy;
Free them from the hand of the wicked.
They do not know, nor do they understand;
They walk about in darkness;
All the foundations of the earth are unstable.
I said, "You are gods,
And all of you are children of the Most High.
But you shall die like men,
And fall like one of the princes."
Arise, O God, judge the earth;
For You shall inherit all nations.

I marvel at Your immensity Lord. Presiding over the universe, You sit in the throne of absolute sovereignty. Yet you are not remote or removed. Your heart is touched by our feelings; Your eyes are open to our predicaments; Your arms are outstretched to support the weak and the unknown. You are the great God of the little people.—SB

Let Them Know

Do not keep silent, O God!
Do not hold Your peace, and do not be still, O Go
For behold, Your enemies make a tumult;
And those who hate You have lifted up their head
They have taken crafty counsel against Your peop
And consulted together against Your sheltered one
They have said, "Come, and let us cut them off
from being a nation, that the name of Israel
may be remembered no more."
For they have consulted together with one consent
They form a confederacy against You;
The tents of Edom and the Ishmaelites;
Moab and the Hagarites;
Gebal, Ammon, and Amalek;
Philistia with the inhabitants of Tyre;
Assyria also has joined with them;
They have helped the children of Lot.   Selah
Deal with them as with Midian, as with Sisera,
As with Jabin at the Brook Kishon,
Who perished at Endor,
Who became as refuse on the earth.
Make their nobles like Oreb and like Zeeb,
Yes, all their princes like Zebah and Zalmunna,
Who said, "Let us take for ourselves
The pastures of God for a possession."
O my God, make them like the whirling dust,
Like the chaff before the wind!
As the fire burns the woods,
And as the flame sets the mountains on fire,
So pursue them with Your tempest,
And frighten them with Your storm.
Fill their faces with shame,
That they may seek Your name, O LORD.
Let them be confounded and dismayed forever;
Yes, let them be put to shame and perish,
That men may know that You,
whose name alone is the LORD,
Are the Most High over all the earth.

*Sometimes I get nervous about the
apparent triumph of evil and Your
apparent silence, Lord. I want You to do
something, not in order that the wicked
might suffer, but to ensure that mankind
does not become confused about Your
majesty. So speak, Lord, to preserve Your
integrity and to banish man's ignorance
of You.—SB*

Blessed is the man
whose strength is in You, whose heart
is set on pilgrimage. As they pass through
the Valley of Baca, they make it a spring;
the rain also covers it with pools.
Every one of them appears
before God
in Zion.

A Place Near Your Altar

How lovely is Your tabernacle, O Lord of hosts!
My soul longs, yes, even faints for the courts
of the LORD;
My heart and my flesh cry out for the living God,
Even the sparrow has found a home,
And the swallow a nest for herself,
Where she may lay her young—
Even Your altars, O LORD of hosts,
My King and my God.
Blessed are those who dwell in Your house;
They will still be praising you.   Selah
Blessed is the man whose strength is in You,
Whose heart is set on pilgrimage.
As they pass through the Valley of Baca,
They make. it a spring;
The rain also covers it with pools.
They go from strength to strength;
Every one of them appears before God in Zion.
O LORD God of hosts, hear my prayer;
Give ear, O God of Jacob!   Selah
O God, behold our shield,
And look upon the face of Your anointed.
For a day in Your courts is better than a thousand.
I would rather be a doorkeeper in the house of my God
Than dwell in the tents of wickedness.
For the LORD God is a sun and shield;
The LORD will give grace and glory;
No good thing will He withhold
From those who walk uprightly.
O LORD of hosts,
Blessed is the man who trusts in You!

Baca is not a literal valley, but speaks of any
place of tears. Prayer offered in the house of
God, or on the altar of our hearts, turns the
place of tears into a well-spring of life, lending
us strength for the days ahead.—jb

Surely His Salvation is Near

Lord, You have been favorable to Your land;
You have brought back the captivity of Jacob.
You have forgiven the iniquity of Your people;
You have covered all their sin.   Selah
You have taken away all Your wrath;
You have turned from the fierceness of Your anger.
Restore us, O God of our salvation,
And cause Your anger toward us to cease.
Will You be angry with us forever?
Will You prolong Your anger to all
generations?
Will You not revive us again.
That Your people may rejoice in You?
Show us Your mercy, O LORD,
And grant us Your salvation.
I will hear what God the LORD will speak,
For He will speak peace to his people
and to His saints,
But let them not turn back to folly.
Surely His salvation is near to those
who fear Him,
That glory may dwell in our land.
Mercy and truth have met together;
Righteousness and peace have kissed each other.
Truth shall spring out of the earth,
And righteousness shall look down from heaven.
Yes, the LORD will give what is good;
And our land will yield its increase.
Righteousness will go before Him,
And shall make His footsteps our pathway.

Aren't you glad God is not a "forever angry"
God? Yet some men are "forever angry" men!
God waived His right to be permanently
annoyed with us—kissing peace that we might
know the breath of love. He can cool our hot
heads and change our angry hearts—if we let
Him!—JB

Teach Me Your Way

Bow down Your ear, O LORD, hear me;
For I am poor and needy.
Preserve my life, for I am holy; You are my God;
Save Your servant who trusts in You!
Be merciful to me, O Lord,
For I cry to You all day long. . . .
For You, Lord, are good, and ready to forgive,
And abundant in mercy to all those who
call upon You. Give ear, O LORD, to my prayer;
And attend to the voice of my supplications.
In the day of my trouble I will call upon You,
For You will answer me.
Among the gods there is none like You, O Lord;
Nor are there any works like Your works.
All nations whom You have made shall come
and worship before You, O Lord,
and shall glorify Your name. For You are great,
and do wondrous things; You alone are God.
Teach me Your way, O LORD;
I will walk in Your truth;
Unite my heart to fear Your name.
I will praise You, O Lord my God, with all my he
And I will glorify Your name forevermore.
For great is Your mercy toward me,
And You have delivered my soul
from the depths of Sheol.
O God, the proud have risen against me,
And a mob of violent men have sought my life,
And have not set You before them. But You, O Lo
are a God full of compassion and gracious,
Longsuffering and abundant in mercy and truth.
Oh, turn to me, and have mercy on me!
Give Your strength to Your servant,
and save the son of Your maidservant.
Show me a sign for good,
That those who hate me may see it and be ashame
Because You, LORD, have helped me
and comforted me.

*There is no shortage of people
propagating programs. Peddlers of
philosophies abound. But I want Your
way, Lord. Theories about God and man,
life and death, flourish on every hand.
But I want to know your direction, to
heed your commands, to live by Your
promises. So reach out of heaven to me,
Lord, and daily teach me Your way.*—SB

You led
Your people like a flock
by the hand of Moses and
Aaron.

Sing aloud to God our strength;
Make a joyful shout to the God of Jacob.
Raise a song and strike the timbrel, the pleasant
harp with the lute. Blow the trumpet at the time
of the New Moon, at the full moon, on our solemn feast day.
For this is a statute for Israel, and a law of the God
of Jacob. This he established in Joseph
for a testimony, when he went through
the land of Egypt, where I heard
a language that I did not understand.